Original title:
Berry Brilliance

Copyright © 2025 Creative Arts Management OÜ
All rights reserved.

Author: Dante Kingsley
ISBN HARDBACK: 978-1-80586-318-2
ISBN PAPERBACK: 978-1-80586-790-6

The Taste of Morning Dew

I woke up with dreams of sweetness,
An orchard alive with fitness.
Dew drops danced upon my tongue,
A fruity tune that's forever sung.

Each bite bursts like a playful prank,
Juice slips down, a slippery flank.
Sunshine giggles in every seed,
A fruit salad's the heart's true need.

Secrets of the Orchard

Whispers float through tangled vines,
Silly squirrels in fruity lines.
Each berry hides a secret bright,
Mischief masked in summer's light.

Laughter lingers in the air,
As sweet surprises fill the fair.
Nature tosses fruit confetti,
In this orchard, things get petty.

Delicate Threads of Flavor

In every layer, a folly spun,
Threads of sweet, oh what fun!
Fruits play dress-up in the sun,
Tangled flavors, a vibrant run.

Tasting joy with every crunch,
Colors swirl, a fruiting bunch.
Tickle your palate, have a laugh,
With juicy jesters, share the craft.

Chasing Sunset's Hues

Under skies that blush and sway,
Fruits in colors chase the day.
A game of tag with juicy fun,
As twilight shimmers, day is done.

Spilling sweetness, laughter grows,
In sunset's light, mischief flows.
Hands stained red, a badge of joy,
A fruity party for every boy.

Juicy Hues of Summer

Beneath the sun, the fruits all grin,
Juicy on the outside, silly within.
Red, blue, and purple, they dance in a line,
Sticky fingers guarantee a good time.

Pies and tarts, oh what a sight,
Jiggle and wobble, oh what a delight!
Nature's sweetness beckons with glee,
Who knew fruit could be so carefree?

Whispers of Wildfruit

In the garden, secrets abound,
Ripe whispers echo from the ground.
Plump little orbs, with a wink and a nod,
Making dessert feel like a game of charades!

Squirrels conspire, they take all the loot,
Stealing our treasures, oh what a hoot!
Nature's jesters, both clever and bold,
With every nibble, their stories unfold.

Nature's Sweet Gems

Clusters of colors, like jewels untamed,
Nature's own bling, none are ashamed.
Poking their heads out, like dapper old gents,
Even the bees seem to offer their compliments.

Fields of laughter, where flavors collide,
Taste tests are riotous; we'll take it all in stride.
With squishy surprises and laughter to share,
Who knew these gems would give us such flair?

Vibrant Harvest Dreams

In vibrant fields, we gleefully roam,
Harvesting maybe a bit more than home.
Jams and jellies, oh, how they spread,
Making toast giggle, it's laughter ahead!

Zany fruit salads, a rainbow delight,
Confetti of flavors, oh what a sight!
Each bite is a dance, a funny little scheme,
Together we savor our harvest dream!

The Blossom's Secret

In a garden where giggles bloom,
Petals whisper secrets of doom.
A strawberry's grin, a blueberry's laugh,
They plot a juicy sneaky path.

Raspberry razzle, a mischievous game,
Hiding from spiders, oh what a shame!
With a wink and a wink, they roll in delight,
Bouncing 'round corners, what a funny sight!

Harvesting Joy from the Earth

Farmers dance with pipes of green,
Gathering fruits like a well-oiled machine.
Cherries chuckle as they dangle low,
While peaches and plums have their own show.

Laughter echoes through the patch,
As they plan a pie—what a match!
They toss the fruit with gleeful cheer,
Saying, 'Come join us, the party's here!'

The Language of Juiciness

Words of sweetness swirl around,
In every fruit, laughter is found.
A kiwi whispers, 'Let's share a laugh,'
While the bananas show their silly half.

Talking in colors, a bright little crew,
Pineapples giggle, 'We're party fruits too!'
Mangoes share smiles, juicy and wide,
In this fruity world, fun cannot hide!

Morning's Garden Serenade

Awake to the choir of fruit-filled delight,
Singing with sunshine, we bask in the light.
Strawberries sway to a zesty tune,
While melons hum softly, morning's boon.

Berry buddies dance on a branch,
Each little shake, a comical chance.
To sway on the breeze, they leap and they twirl,
In a morning garden, laughter's the pearl.

Nectar of the Land

Juicy jewels hang on vines,
A feast of colors so divine.
They giggle as you take a bite,
A splash of sweetness, pure delight.

Their laughter echoes through the trees,
Dancing about in summer's breeze.
Wobbling, juggling, slip and slide,
The fruit parade takes us for a ride!

The Short-lived Joy

A bright red splash, oh what a sight,
But one quick munch, they take flight.
Smashed in my pocket, all in a rush,
Those sweet little snacks turn into mush.

Oh, how they laugh when I complain,
"Eat us slowly, don't be insane!"
But the sweetness whispers, "Just one more,"
Then they vanish, leaving me wanting more.

Harvesting Dreams

In fields of green, we gather round,
Laughter erupts from the fruit-filled ground.
With baskets full and smiles wide,
We race for glory, side by side.

Each pluck ignites a candy burst,
A joyous snack that quenches thirst.
But watch your step or you'll slip,
And join the chaos with a flip!

Laughter in the Fields

Giggling fruits among the leaves,
Their silly dance makes us believe.
That every bite is a comedy show,
With fruity punchlines, oh the flow!

In every patch, a joke appears,
The juiciest puns bring us to cheers.
So gather round, let's have some fun,
In this fruity fest, we've already won!

The Enchantment of Earthly Delights

In gardens where the laughter grows,
Fruits wear shoes and dance in rows.
Strawberries juggle, they're quite bold,
While blueberries tell tales of old.

Raspberries play chess with the peas,
And maraschinos swing in the breeze.
Bananas slip on the grassy floor,
Oh, these delights, who could ask for more?

Cherries wear hats that are way too big,
Getting stuck in a grape's little jig.
Pineapples wear sunglasses so bright,
In this fruity world, everything feels right.

With every bite, a giggle escapes,
A carnival of colors, a feast of shapes.
Taste buds dancing, a fruity ballet,
In this joyous garden, let's laugh and play!

Melodies of Noteworthy Fruits

Apples sing in harmony sweet,
While oranges tap dance with their feet.
Kiwis strum on a vine-made lute,
And plums in tuxedos join the loot.

Grapes giggle with each little squash,
As mangos compete to make a big splash.
Lemons whistle tunes so sour and bright,
In the orchestra of flavors, oh what a sight!

Papayas spin tales of sun-kissed lanes,
While peaches arrange their sweet refrains.
Every fruit has a part to play,
In this musical field where we laugh all day.

So let's join this fruity parade,
With juicy notes that never fade.
In this concert of joy, feel the cheer,
For who doesn't love fruit that sings in the sphere?

The Savor of Twilight Gardens

Under the stars, where night takes hold,
Fruits gather for stories yet untold.
A cantaloupe tells knock-knock jokes,
While elderflowers giggle with the folks.

In the twilight, the figs wear ties,
And each raspberry has big dreams to rise.
They compete for the best sparkle and glow,
As the moonlight makes their colors show.

Peaches sip nectar from sleepy blooms,
As nighttime fun dispels all glooms.
A symphony of flavors, they share,
In this night garden, without a care.

Come join our feast beneath the boughs,
Where laughter erupts, and joy allows.
With each sweet bite, let out a cheer,
For the evening's magic is finally here!

Quintessential Fruit Lullabies

In a cradle of leaves, the fruits hum low,
Bananas in pajamas steal the show.
Apples sway with a gentle ballet,
As cherries giggle the night away.

Watermelons cast shadows so wide,
As grapefruits snore with a sweet pride.
Lemons dream in their zesty homes,
While berries play tag in their colorful domes.

Pineapples croon their cozy tunes,
Under a sky that's dotted with moons.
Every fruit drifts in dreams so tender,
With laughter and love, their sweet splendor.

So close your eyes, let the laughter soar,
In this fruit-filled world, let your heart explore.
With fruity lullabies floating on air,
Dream of delights that are utterly rare!

Nature's Hidden Splendor

In the garden, fruits conspire,
Wobbling softly, dancing higher.
Bouncing berries, round and sweet,
Squeezing smiles from every beet.

A cheerful crew in red and blue,
Giggling loud, among the dew.
Each little blob, a joyful tease,
Chasing ants with sticky knees.

The Tantalizing Taste of Dawn

Morning rays, they light the spree,
Biting fruit as bright as glee.
Sipping sunshine in a cup,
Waking sleepy taste buds up.

Jelly on toast, it's quite the spread,
Wobbling winks, bringing cheer instead.
With every munch, a laugh's ahoy,
Flavors bouncing, purest joy.

Symphony of Tangy Temptations

Strawberries giggle, raspberries sing,
Twirling together in a fruity fling.
Crisp little munches, a crunchy delight,
Popping confetti with every bite.

Harmony swells in a colorful bowl,
Berries bouncing, that's the goal!
A joyful mess from every cheer,
Splattered giggles just appear.

Colors in a Bowl of Dreams

Hold the bowl filled to the brim,
These happy fruits make senses swim.
Purple, red, and yellow bright,
Singing songs of sheer delight.

Fruit salad tango, a jolly dance,
Every scoop heightens the chance.
To taste the fun, you must dive deep,
In this bowl, laughter sleeps.

A Symphony of Tart and Sweet

In the garden, chaos reigns,
Tiny fruits dance, dodging rains.
Raspberries bursting with glee,
Sour faces, oh so funny!

Blueberries plop like little balls,
Splatting down from fevered falls.
Strawberries flaunt their red, bold flair,
While all giggle at their pair!

The tartness meets sweet in the bowl,
A riotous blend that makes us whole.
Pies and jams, what a sight,
Let's munch until we can't feel right!

Laughter echoes with each fresh taste,
In this fruity world, there's no waste.
Cherries chuckle, they can't believe,
How much joy they can achieve!

Garden's Burst of Color

In the patch where colors clash,
Red and blue in a playful splash.
They poke their heads from leafy beds,
A fruity circus fills our heads!

Blackberries boast with juicy pride,
While green leaves tease them, side by side.
Limes roll over, acting sly,
Oh, what a mess, oh my, oh my!

With yellow lemons looking shocked,
And purple grapes, they're all unlocked.
A rainbow riot in the sun,
Each pluck a giggle, what fun begun!

We grab a basket, off we go,
Laughing as we sway to and fro.
In this garden, pure delight,
Colors burst, and hearts take flight!

The Flavorful Canvas

On a canvas bright and wide,
Colors mingle, side by side.
Painted hues, splashy and bold,
The flavor tales begin to unfold.

Pinks and reds play tag and run,
Giggling softly, oh what fun!
Slice a pear, paint it green,
Every bite a taste unseen!

Peaches tickle, nectar flows,
With every scoop, the laughter grows.
Mix it up in wild delight,
This art of fruits is a pure sight!

Creativity served on a plate,
Who can say what's worth the rate?
Join the feast, don't hesitate,
For every flavor seals our fate!

Fragrant Promises of Yield

In the breeze, sweet scents arise,
Hints of fruit, a bold surprise.
Rhubarb waves with its tangy grin,
Inviting us to dive right in!

Honeydew whispers, 'try a bite',
While cantaloupe shimmers in the light.
Each scent a promise, oh, so bright,
Planting laughter in every sight.

Apples tumble down the lane,
Silly games in this fruity chain.
Peaches roll, giggling with flair,
Silly dances float in the air!

As we gather this harvest bright,
Laughter spills under the twilight.
In this field, we find our yield,
Fragrant dreams in every field!

Luscious Fields of Delight

In the fields so bright and bold,
The fruits of laughter unfold.
Bouncing berries, round and sweet,
Playing tag with tiny feet.

Sunshine smiles upon the vines,
As jiggly jellies form in lines.
A dance of colors, all a-flare,
Nature's sweets beyond compare.

The Artistry of Garden Abundance

A painter splashes colors here,
In gardens filled with cheer.
Strawberry hats and blueberry ties,
Cranberries wink with twinkly eyes.

Brush strokes of green, red, and blue,
Nature's palette, fresh and new.
Potato chips dance on the grass,
As broccoli giggles—what a sass!

Sweet Simplicity in Nature's Palette

Simple joys, just look and see,
Raspberries giggle, wild and free.
Grape-sorcerers cast a spell,
Wrapping sweetness like a shell.

Fruity hats and juicy shoes,
Wear your flavors; you can't lose!
With every munch, a funny cheer,
Nature's jokes are crystal clear.

Glories of the Orchard's Heart

In the orchard, joy abounds,
Where silly laughter spins around.
Apple pies do flips and spins,
Peachy giggles, where the fun begins.

Cherries burst with laughter bright,
As pears engage in playful fights.
Nature's bounty gleefully shares,
A feast of giggles, who would dare?

Dappled Sunlight on Ripened Harvest

Underneath the leafy crown,
Berries blushing, no one frowns.
Sunshine dapples, a cheeky tease,
Nature's jester, put us at ease.

Chasing shadows, we laugh and run,
Ripened treats, oh, what fun!
With every bite, a giggle flies,
Sweet surprises in every guise.

Juicy Secrets beneath the Canopy

Beneath the leaves, the whispers grow,
Juicy tales, in sunlit glow.
Wink at the bushes, shhhh, don't shout,
Secret flavors hiding out.

Raspberry giggles, blueberry schemes,
Plotting sweet, absurd daydreams.
Let's not tell the farmers any lies,
These fruits hold magic in disguise.

The Dance of Red and Blue

Red winks at blue in a fruity tango,
Twisting and turning, a berry fandango.
Flavors collide, they sway and sway,
Who leads the dance? No one can say!

Laughter echoes across the patch,
Bouncing berries with a playful catch.
One goes left, the other spins fast,
In this wild waltz, who'll have the last laugh?

Enchanted Fields of Flavor

In fields of charm where colors play,
Fruits plot pranks in a jolly way.
A strawberry giggles, a grape rolls wide,
In this land of taste, there's nothing to hide.

The sun shines sly, the breeze joins in,
A berry party, let the games begin!
With every munch, our laughter takes flight,
In enchanted fields, joy feels just right.

Bountiful Kisses from Nature

Under a bush, something's peeking,
Red and round, it's just squeaking.
A little critter takes a bite,
What a mess, oh what a sight!

Juicy stains on tiny paws,
Nature's gifts without a pause.
Laughing loudly, we share a snack,
Nature's treasures on the track!

Sunshine sparkles, sweet delight,
With every nibble, hearts take flight.
So tasty wild, so bold, so bright,
Nature's kisses, pure delight!

Waltzing through the fields so wide,
With silly hats, we take a ride.
Chasing sweetness, oh so grand,
Nature's kisses, hand in hand!

Nature's Sweet Child

Little seeds in soil do giggle,
When spring arrives — they dance and wiggle.
Out pops a sprout, the sun's warm gaze,
Nature's child in a green bouquet.

Rolling hills are home for fun,
Where plump delights bask in the sun.
With gummies hanging from each vine,
Sweetness waiting for us to dine!

Frogs leap in delight nearby,
Chasing bugs as they jump high.
Nature's child, with glee we cheer,
Snacking laughters fill the year!

Piglets join in, snouts so cute,
Snuffling berries, oh so astute!
Cheeky bites, giggles that spring,
Nature's sweet child, what joy they bring

Tasting the Essence of Earth

In a patch where giggles roam,
We pluck some fruits to take them home.
Tiny hands all sticky, oh,
Taste of sunshine, let it flow!

Picking berries with glee and hops,
Jumping high, never gonna stop!
For every squish, there's lots of laughs,
Munching joy in simple drafts.

Sour, sweet, or juicy sprays,
Tasting life in many ways.
Nature's flavors in a row,
Makes our happy faces glow!

With each bite, a joke we find,
Tickled pink, we're intertwined.
Tasting earth, pure silly cheer,
Every nibble, bright and clear!

A Radiant Collection of Nature's Bounty

A treasure hunt in fields so bright,
Searching for goodness, what a sight!
With baskets clinking, smiles so wide,
We gather gifts the earth does provide.

Splashes of colors, oh what a show,
Tiny treasures in rows bestow.
Laughter erupts, a joyful cheer,
For every pluck, we draw near!

A tapestry of flavors bold,
Stories in each fruit unfold.
Mirth and mischief in every bite,
Nature's bounty, pure delight!

Join the party — come and see,
Wiggling worms giggle with glee.
A radiant feast for all to share,
Silly moments, beyond compare!

Sunkissed Dreams on Petals

Beneath the sun, in nature's dress,
The bees do dance, without a stress.
A strawberry hat, I wear with glee,
Pronouncing loudly, 'Look at me!'

In shades of red, bright as a fire,
Silly thoughts that never tire.
With every nibble, smiles abound,
Joyously laughing, then falling down.

Softly squished on my shirt so fine,
I say, 'Guys, it's laundry time!'
Who knew that fun could leave a mark?
Berry stains dance in the park!

With laughter bright and sunbeams warm,
I'll chase the critters, help them swarm.
In this merry mess, let it be known,
Nature's wonders turn us to stone!

The Lure of Nature's Nectar

A glistening red, like a ruby jewel,
Out in the field, where's the ghoul?
I'll climb a tree, in search of bliss,
For a fruit that could lead to a kiss!

Oh, how the birds do seem to laugh,
As I chase them round, and I start to gasp.
They know the spots where sweets do lay,
While I'm tripping over rows of hay!

So sweet the taste, it makes me dance,
In sticky shoes, oh how I prance.
I'm a berry bandit, that's my creed,
With all my friends, share this wild deed!

Yet nature's nectar can lead astray,
My tummy says, 'Maybe just one more play!'
But giggles echo through the trees,
On this silly hunt, I'm truly free!

Fruits of the Forgotten Path

Down the lane where wild things grow,
I trip on roots, saying, 'Whoa!'
Hidden treasures, bursting bright,
I grab a handful, what a sight!

Each plump bite, a giggle feast,
Nature whispers, 'You're the beast!'
A berry crown upon my head,
With wild delights, I laugh instead!

But watch your steps, my clumsy friend,
For every giggle could soon end.
I tumble down, and so do they,
We're all just fruit in disarray!

At last, we feast on juicy spoils,
With sticky fingers, making noise.
I shout, 'This path is worth the risk!'
With berry magic, it's hard to miss!

Luscious Echoes of the Woods

In woodland shadows, spirits play,
With plump delights to steal away.
Giggles float on lilac air,
As we discover our fruity lair.

With whispered secrets from the trees,
We sing to squirrels, 'Oh, please, oh please!'
Red and round, they burst with cheer,
Dancing with critters, what a frontier!

Berry joy in the crisp, cool shade,
Squeezed between laughter, plans we laid.
'Watch this!' I shout, and trip, oh no!
Nature chuckles, puts on a show!

Yet as we nibble on nature's cheer,
Every bite draws us near.
With echoes of laughter, wild and free,
These luscious woods are home to me!

The Dance of Ruby Juices

In a bowl, they waltz, bright and bold,
Twisting and turning, never quite old.
Juicy little gems, in a sweet parade,
Tickling our taste buds, a vibrant charade.

With a plop and a squish, they make quite a mess,
Rolling around like they're wearing a dress.
A laughter erupts as they hop and they play,
Who knew such fruit could steal the day?

Oh, watch them jive under the sun's warm gaze,
Twirling in smoothies, they set us ablaze.
They spill out their secrets with every squeeze,
Partaking in mischief, they dance with ease.

In pies and tarts, they strut their stuff,
Taking our tastebuds on a ride that's tough.
A fruity jamboree, a celebratory feast,\nWith every fresh bite, our joy is released.

Hidden Treasures in the Field

Down in the grass, where the wild things grow,
Little gems of sweetness, all in a row.
Some are hiding, some peeking through,
A treasure hunt waiting, just for me and you.

With hands like detectives, we search high and low,
Finding these wonders, with eyes all aglow.
They giggle and splash, when picked from their nest,
Nature's little treats, a delightful quest.

While neighbors all wonder, what's all the fuss,
We're munching on goodness, just us and our dust.
Stains on our fingers, laughs in the air,
Who thought these small fruits would be such a dare?

In the end, we gather, our basket so bright,
A rainbow of laughter, a delicious sight.
Winking at us, with their mischievous sheen,
These hidden delights rule the field like a queen.

The Color of Ripeness

A riot of hues, oh what a display,
When fruits are ripe, they simply sway.
Like toddlers in the sun, they giggle with glee,
Bursting with flavor, wild and free.

Red like a clown's nose, sweet and round,
They boast of their charm, a joy profound.
Each little bite, a jolly delight,
Painting our palates with colors so bright.

Whispers of laughter sip through the air,
As we munch on the fun, without a care.
The stage is set for a flavor parade,
In a silly game, no fruit must fade.

So let's grab a handful, and let out a cheer,
For this play of hues, brings everyone near.
In every sweet morsel, a story is spun,
In the colorful world, we all become one.

Sunlit Fields of Flavor

Beneath the warm sun, they frolic and roll,
In fields of flavor, they reach for the goal.
A giggly reminder, with every small taste,
That life is delicious, never a waste.

Merry little crops, frolicking freely,
In nature's playground, adventurous and cheeky.
With laughter that bounces, and joy that spills,
Each sunny nibble brings magical thrills.

They bounce on the breeze, like kids at play,
Crafting a feast in their own fruity way.
As shadows dance lightly, we gather around,
These sunlit sweets, in laughter abound.

So here's to the fields, where flavors collide,
In every sunbeam, pure happiness resides.
With a wink and a grin, we dive into cheer,
For the joy of the harvest, is splendidly clear.

Threads of Sweetness in the Breeze

In the garden, giggles bloom,
With fruits that chase away the gloom.
Mischief hangs on every vine,
A jester's secret in the brine.

Cherries wear their little hats,
While raspberries tease sneaky cats.
A strawberry starts a dance so bright,
Under the sun, oh what a sight!

Blueberries whisper silly dreams,
As they float in sugary streams.
Each fruit a prankster, bouncing free,
Crafting glee in harmony.

In the breeze, laughter's found,
With every squish and every sound.
A sweet parade on nature's stage,
Where the fruity jesters engage.

The Colorful Poetry of the Garden

In hues of red, the vibes ignite,
Strawberry giggles in the light.
Raspberry rhymes in clumps they cling,
Listen close, hear the laughter ring.

A blueberry brigade rolling by,
Wearing crowns, oh my, oh my!
Peeking from leaves, they plot and scheme,
Creating a berry-filled dream.

Blackberries high-five from the vine,
Scribbling verses, oh so fine.
Juicy secrets they can share,
In a world of fruity flair.

Every color spouts a jest,
In the garden, we are blessed.
With every fruit, a hint of fun,
A colorful play, never done.

Secrets Held in Succulent Moments

In a bowl of laughter, I see the game,
Each fruit a star, none ever lame.
With smooth, shiny skins, they conspire,
To tickle our tongues and never tire.

The grapes giggle, sweet and round,
Hiding secrets without a sound.
A pop, a burst, and then they flee,
Leaving tastes that dance with glee.

Plucking treasures, we taste the fun,
Painting smiles under the sun.
Juicy tales in every bite,
Crafting memories, sheer delight.

Moments are sweeter when shared around,
With fruity joys, laughter's found.
Each nibble brings a chuckle bright,
In the glow of pure delight.

A Tapestry of Sweetness

Woven whispers in fields of cheer,
Fruits in layers, come gather near.
Mirthful moments stitched with zest,
In juicy threads, we find our quest.

Tangles of flavors, playful games,
Every bite ignites new names.
From the bushes, a vivid spree,
Colors flash like a jubilee.

Pies are born with giggles galore,
Merry chefs, creating more.
These treats, delightful in their form,
In laughter's arms, we keep warm.

A tart embrace, a sugary kiss,
In the garden, we find our bliss.
This tapestry of life unfurls,
Where joyous sweetness twirls and twirls.

Beneath the Canopy of Boughs

Under leafy hats, we prance,
With giggles and a silly dance.
A squirrel stares with wide-eyed glee,
As we munch snacks beneath the tree.

The sun tickles our noses bright,
While ants parade, a funny sight.
Their tiny legs in marching line,
Steal crumbs from our picnic divine.

A bird drops in, just to tease,
Keen on stealing our cheese please.
We laugh and chase, a comedic scene,
Nature's show, oh what a screen!

With sticky fingers, all aglow,
We dance beneath the boughs that grow.
Adventure calls, a silly choir,
In the green where laughs won't tire.

Luminance of Nature's Palette

Colors splash across the glade,
Where sunbeams frolic, unafraid.
Grass tickles toes, a playful tease,
As we stumble, laughing with ease.

A ladybug in polka dots,
Stands guard on mushrooms, all the spots.
We take a picture, strike a pose,
Next to the flower with the nose!

Fingers painting with bright hues,
Who knew nature had such views?
A vibrant world, alive and round,
Where silly stories can be found.

In this place of funny cheer,
We spin and laugh, no trace of fear.
Nature's canvas, oh what fun!
A gallery for everyone.

The Charms of a Garden's Heart

In the garden, whimsy grows,
Twirling petals in funny shows.
A scarecrow dances with a grin,
While worms wiggle beneath the skin.

Marigolds gossip, petals flapping,
About the gopher who's been napping.
We cheer the bees that buzz and hum,
As butterflies join, oh here they come!

A spoonful of dirt is how we start,
Planting seeds with all our heart.
Then radishes pop up with surprise,
In this cheeky garden of highs.

With watering cans in silly hands,
We splash around in laughter's stands.
The garden's charms we now embrace,
With every giggle, a happy place.

Tasting the Dawn's Embrace

Morning dew like fruity tea,
A sippy cup for birds and me.
With sleepy yawns and cozy socks,
We nibble toast with jelly blocks.

Sunrise bursts with colors bright,
Tickling our dreams in soft light.
A toaster pops with joyful 'ping!'
As we munch on this morning fling.

Frogs croak tunes from the nearby bog,
Their morning croon, a lazy log.
Butterflies flutter, full of cheer,
As we lick jam without fear.

The day unfolds with silly taste,
As we explore with no time to waste.
In the morning's whimsical embrace,
Every moment is a hopping chase.

Sweet Elegance of Summer

In the sun's warm embrace, we dance,
Juicy gems in a grassy expanse.
Plump treasures glisten, red and bright,
With smiles that spark in summer's light.

A toddler's giggle, a splash of juice,
Sticky hands from the wild produce.
Laughter echoes, sweet fruits collide,
A revelry, where joy can't hide.

In picnic blankets, we take our place,
With fruity chaos, a wild embrace.
As ants join the feast without a ask,
We giggle and munch, it's a sticky task.

Fingers stained, an artistic mess,
Each bite a burst, nothing less.
A summer without it just wouldn't do,
Sweet laughter and fruit, a perfect brew.

The Vibrant Palette of the Orchard

In orchards where the painters play,
Pinks and purples gleam all day.
Each droplet wears a radiant crown,
Fruity fun that won't let you frown.

A splash of color on your shirt,
A moment's glee, a bit of dirt.
The trees stand tall, like wacky crew,
With fruits that dream of paintbrushes too.

We climb and jump, not bound by rules,
Sampling sweetness like little fools.
With every mouthful, giggles ensue,
Oh, what a canvas, painted in hue!

Let's not forget our berry quest,
In nature's stall, we find the best.
With laughter echoing through the grove,
In this vibrant maze, we sweetly rove.

Tiny Treasures of the Thicket

In the thicket where mischief resides,
Tiny treasures in nature's hides.
A plump surprise in every nook,
With critters peeking, a curious look.

Jam-packed bushes, a playful spree,
Flinging fruit and climbing a tree.
The whispers of leaves, a giggly tease,
While squishy delights dance on the breeze.

We gather our spoils, our silly loot,
With berry crowns, oh, what a hoot!
The thicket's bounty, wild and free,
Turns into a feast, just you and me.

Wandering through with sticky pride,
Side by side with laughter wide.
In our little kingdom, sweet and spry,
We find magic where the small things lie.

The Whisper of Wild Harvest

When morning dew paints the earth anew,
Whispering secrets that nature drew.
A clamor of joy amidst leafy green,
With surprises popping, a merry scene.

Hands outstretched, we scavenge wide,
Each plump delight we can't abide.
The giggles echo, a silly call,
As we bounce and tumble and drop the haul.

Invisible fairies sprinkle delight,
As fruits hang low, a tempting sight.
We weave through the patches, a playful nest,
With wild-eyed laughter in this happy quest.

Soon, we feast on our harvest bold,
Stories shared, so sweetly told.
In nature's banquet, we find our bliss,
With fruity giggles, who could resist?

Nature's Silken Desserts

In gardens galore, fruits sway and tease,
They giggle with whispers, rustling with ease.
A strawberry's grin, bright red and round,
Winks at the passerby, jolly and proud.

Raspberries giggle, titter and tumble,
While curious bees add to the rumble.
Blueberries bounce, a carnival dance,
Inviting all critters to join in their prance.

In the pie's company, they start to croon,
Singing sweet anthems, oh what a tune!
They plot mischief, a tart little jest,
Who knew fruits could party, they're truly the best!

And when night falls, with a wink and a cheer,
These fruits begin tales that all can hear.
As the moon smiles down on their jolly ballet,
Nature's desserts keep the boredom at bay.

Earth's Sweet Exclamations

A cherry on top, with a hat made of cream,
Shouts, "Look at me!" in a sugary dream.
The fruits have a forum, all colors and shapes,
Debating their flavors, new lines and new japes.

"Who's juiciest here?" a grapearian cries,
While a mango, all yellow, just quietly sighs.
The orange leaps up, shouting, "I'm zest!
Watch out, my friends, I've passed every test!"

Blackberries tumble, a clumsy brigade,
Accusing the blueberries of being too staid.
They trip on their jokes, weaving laughs on the vine,
In the fruit bowl of laughter, they all intertwine.

As sunlight filters through cracks in the wall,
The fruits play their games, having a ball.
With each bite taken, a giggle is tossed,
In Earth's sweet theatrics, no flavor is lost.

Succulent Scenes of Pure Joy

A picnic unfolds on a patchwork quilt,
Where swirls of delight in a berry are built.
Sliced fruit in a bowl, a colorful show,
They conspire with laughter, putting on a glow.

Grapes wear their hats, so pompous, so fine,
While pie crusts are giggling, outshining the wine.
"Let's dance on the plates!" the muffins all cheer,
As whipped cream sings duets, delightful to hear.

They toss around puns like seeds in the breeze,
Relishing every joke, tickled with ease.
Lemon's remarks are tart, yet sincere,
While kiwi just rolls, "I'm the best snack here!"

In a world full of color, laughter prevails,
With blushing ripe fruits sharing their tales.
No frowns allowed in this jubilant game,
In joy's juicy playground, they've made a name.

Luscious Melodies of the Forest

Deep in the woods, where the sunlight streams,
Fruits gather around to share zany dreams.
"Let's form a band!" cries a wild berry cheek,
With nuts as the strings, they play hide-and-seek.

Mushrooms hum bass, while the leaves keep the beat,
Nature's odd orchestra, quite hard to defeat.
Rascally radishes try to join in,
With carrots on drums, what a whimsical din!

They swish and they swash, a rhythm divine,
Berries harmonize, each sweetly aligned.
A raspberry solo, oh what a delight,
Every note's draped in a soft evening light.

As twilight descends on their musical spree,
The fruits laugh together, all wild and free.
In the forest of flavor, no one's ever solo,
For laughter and music make life a grand show.

Reflections of Crimson and Azure

In a garden where colors collide,
Fruits play hide and seek with pride.
Red cheeks giggle in the sun,
Winking at blue, it's all in good fun.

A raspberry blushes, thinks it's a star,
While blueberries claim they've come from afar.
'Look at my hue!' the strawberry brags,
But the blueberry just tugs its green nags.

They dance on the vine, a lively parade,
Each hue upstaging, like they were made.
The laughter echoes, a frenzied cheer,
Nature's mistake, or a grand souvenir?

So in this riot of color and cheer,
We all know the flavors that draw us near.
With sweetness galore, and blocks of delight,
Life's just a feast—oh what a sight!

Incandescent Flavors of the Wild

In the wild where flavors collide,
Nature's kitchen, open wide.
Peeking out from bushes, a juicy scene,
Lighting up taste buds, so fresh and keen.

An orange slice jokes, 'I'm just a tease!'
While a cheeky grape rolls in with ease.
With laughter bubbling in the air,
Mango offers hugs, so fruity and rare.

Cherries giggle in their cherry red,
Whispering tales that tickle your head.
Each plump little joke in nature's surprise,
Like jester hats worn by colorful pies.

The wild is a feast, a giddy delight,
Where flavors play tag from morning to night.
So grab a spoon, let the games begin,
In this wacky world, everyone wins!

The Circle of Flavor and Fragrance

Gather round in fruit's grand hall,
Where flavors sing and fragrances call.
A circle forms, each one takes a turn,
To share their stories, and for more we yearn.

The elderberry boasts of its ancient fame,
While young blackcurrant plays the silly game.
'Lemonade's my jam!' the citrus prances,
And all join in for fruity advances.

The peach piped up, 'I'm fuzzy, so sweet!'
While grapes roll around on their tiny feet.
Together they laugh, a chorus so bright,
Spilling their secrets from morning to night.

With every giggle, flavors entwine,
In laughter, they twirl like a fruity design.
So find your circle, let flavors take flight,
In this joyful jam of nature's delight!

A Tasting Tour of Nature

Join the tour of nature's fare,
With giggles and smiles hanging in the air.
Each stop a delight, oh what a scene,
With fruity flavors fit for a queen!

First up, a tasting of ripe, red bliss,
Where a strawberry donates a sweet kiss.
Next, juicy orbs with a blueberry cheer,
As flavors unfurl, they bring forth the jeer.

All aboard for this merry parade,
Where each tasty treat is a slice of the grade.
Raspberry shouts, 'I drip with glee!'
As blackberries nudge, 'Don't forget me!'

With spoons in hand, we're ready to munch,
Cranberries bouncing, all set for lunch.
So take a bite, let the laughter ring,
In this playful tour, nature's the king!

Threads of Juicy Reverie

In a garden where colors collide,
Bouncing berries take a wild ride.
Strawberries giggle, blueberries sing,
Rambunctious fruits, what joy they bring!

With a splash of juice, they attempt to fly,
Twirling and whirling, oh my, oh my!
Raspberries rustle, making quite a mess,
A fruity party, what kind of finesse!

Their laughter echoes through the warm air,
Bouncing off bushes without a care.
The stems have got moves, can you believe?
A fabulous frolic, they never leave!

In this patch of whimsy, joy is unbound,
Each berry a jester, jumping around.
With each little nibble, a giggle will bloom,
Come join the fun, let's banish the gloom!

Bonanza of Sweetness

Under the sun, the fruits start to play,
Dancing in baskets, come join their sway!
Mangoes and peaches in a sunny waltz,
Creating a frenzy, it's no one's fault!

Splashing with flavors, they jive out loud.
Making a ruckus, oh, aren't they proud?
Fruits in a frenzy, a carnival dream,
Who knew such chaos could burst at the seam?

As cherries chuckle, the plums roll their eyes,
One by one, they all start to rise.
A top-notch affair of pit and skin,
With each little bite, let the laughter begin!

When the last fruit flops, there's a grand cheer,
A bonanza, indeed, flavor's premier!
Join in the giggles, let sweetness devour,
In this juicy jamboree, it's always our hour!

Radiance of Nature's Collection

Oh, behold the rainbow on the vine,
Fruits flaunting colors, simply divine!
Lemons in laughter, oranges in glee,
A zesty parade, come taste and see!

Pineapples strut in their tropical crowns,
While melons giggle with vibrant frowns.
The fruits are in fashion, ripe to the core,
Each one a masterpiece, who could ask more?

Watermelons rolling with utmost delight,
Bobbing and weaving from left to right.
A harvest of fun in every bright hue,
Nature's collection, an edible view!

As night falls, they sparkle under the moon,
Still laughing and swirling to their own tune.
Join this riot, just grab a plate,
Savor the joy, do not hesitate!

The Flavorful Dance of Sunshine

In the morning light, the fruits take their stand,
Jiving together, hand in hand.
With each little bounce, they cause a delight,
Peaches do cartwheels, wow, what a sight!

With a twirl and a whirl, raspberries cheer,
While citrus fruits giggle, spreading good cheer.
A dance of delight, so fruity and bright,
Lemonade boogies till the fall of night!

Figs flaunt their colors in a grand parade,
Dancing with laughter, never afraid.
The rhythm they bring is simply divine,
Nature's own concert, delightful design!

So grab your crew and join in the fun,
A flavorful dance under the sun!
With giggles and smiles, it's time to prance,
In this fruity fiesta, come take a chance!

The Magic of Edible Art

In a basket, colors collide,
Mismatched socks on a joyride.
Blue and red, a playful scene,
Nature's candies, fit for a queen.

Jellybeans in a berry hat,
One hops away, oh where's it at?
Chasing flavors, quite the quest,
Wanna take a bite? Be my guest!

Splat of jam on my new dress,
Oops, now I'm a sticky mess.
Laughter echoes, sweet and loud,
Art on toast, I'm berry proud!

A fruit parade, they'll sashay,
Dancing in a bright bouquet.
Line up for the tastiest show,
Watch as these delights just glow!

Critters giggle, nibble, munch,
Sipping juice and having brunch.
With every bite, laughter starts,
Creating magic, oh my arts!

Glorious Gems of the Vineyard

Under grapes, we trip and fall,
Laughter rises, hear the call.
A grape on the nose, what a sight,
Can we paint it? Sure, that's right!

Juicy orbs, they light up days,
Rolling down in many ways.
From vine to glass, a wobbly chase,
Stumbling through this fruity place.

Uncork the giggles, let it flow,
Swirling round, a purple show.
Twirling grapes in merry dance,
Join the fun, come take a chance!

With every sip, we grin so wide,
Join the grape stomp, come and slide.
When laughter bubbles, it's a treat,
Dancing hoof to juicy beat!

In the vineyard, joy is the law,
Bright ideas that make you guffaw.
Raise your glass, let's toast tonight,
To grape adventures, pure delight!

Echoes of a Flavorful Journey

A fruity road all twists and turns,
Found a secret, oh how it churns!
Strawberries giggle, tickling my nose,
With every bite, the laughter grows.

Over hills, where berries play,
Racing clouds, a berry ballet.
Pies on bikes, what a wild sight,
Dreamy flavors take to flight!

A jam spill causes giggles wide,
Slip and slide, let's run and hide.
Carts of fruit, a funny ride,
Juicy jars, we can't abide!

Berries chatting, full of sass,
Bouncing round, they race so fast.
Caught in laughter, can't resist,
This fruity journey, pure bliss!

Echoes of laughter, sweet and spry,
As flavors dance, they wave goodbye.
A tale of tangy, fun awaits,
Let's hop aboard—before it rates!

Fables of the Flavorful Fields

In fields where tickled tongues reside,
A story spins, come take a ride.
Flavors whisper, "Here we are!",
Each taste a giggle, every jar.

Watch the squash don a silly grin,
As berries bounce, thick and thin.
Broccoli joined, what a delight,
Dance-off challenge, who's more bright?

Fields of laughter, colors shine,
With every flavor, feelings twine.
Crazy carrots, peas so bold,
Fables of joy, sweetly told.

Rainbow radishes tap their feet,
In this garden, life's a treat.
Picking giggles, that's the game,
Add to the basket, never the same!

So gather 'round, make note of this,
In every crunch, there's an abyss!
From sun to soil, flavors weave,
Stories of laughter, we believe!

Harvest Moon's Temptation

Under the harvest moon's glow,
Fruits dance like stars in a row.
Jelly jars clink, it's quite a sight,
Mice plot their heist late at night.

Cherries giggle, plump and red,
They whisper secrets to the bread.
A pie with a grin, what a delight,
Even the forks are feeling bright.

Crisp autumn air gives a cheer,
Squirrels risk acorns, oh dear!
The mad rush for that last sweet treat,
What a comedy on this fine seat!

With every crumble, laughter rings,
A splash of juice, and someone sings.
The moon watches on, quite amused,
At this joy that can't be confused.

Glimmers of Summer's Bounty

In the garden where chaos reigns,
Tomato plants play silly games.
Zucchini hides, a green charade,
While bees are buzzing in parade.

Strawberries wear polka dot hats,
Rabbits join in, and dance like brats.
Tommy Tater tells wild tales,
As the sunlight paints the trails.

Basil and mint make a cool drink,
Lemon and lime, let's not overthink.
Then someone shouts, a splash, a swirl,
Oh my, it's minty-greens with a twirl!

We toast to flavors and spices so bright,
While cucumbers giggle, quite a sight.
Silly veggies, it's all in good fun,
As summer ends and we're on the run.

Ripe Reflections in Morning Dew

Dew drops sparkle on the leaves,
A nudge to snooze, as nature weaves.
Peaches blush, a silent jest,
While parrots plot their breakfast quest.

Blueberries with their tiny hats,
Sway to tunes from nearby bats.
Lemons chirp with zestful sound,
As each fruit performs underground.

Marshmallow clouds float in the sky,
While grapes gossip and float nearby.
"Who's got the best color?" they croon,
Contemplating glory by the moon.

Morning giggles, a fresh delight,
As fruit and nature join in the fight.
A banquet spread for all to see,
In the dewy dawn, wild and free.

Mosaic of Flavor and Fragrance

In a bowl of colors, oh what a sight,
Fruits play cards, bringing delight.
Kiwi winks, with sly little charm,
While oranges tease with citrus alarm.

Apples crack jokes with crunchy delight,
Pineapple bursts in a fruity fight.
"Who's the juiciest of us?" they ask,
With laughter behind every task.

Raspberry raves in a sweet pink dress,
While grapes giggle, "We're all blessed!"
As they toss from bowl to bowl, you see,
The fun of flavors, wild and free.

In this fruity burst of joy we partake,
Not a single fruit dares to fake.
With every scoop, we toss and cheer,
Mosaic smiles, deliciously clear.

Sipping on Sunshine

A glass of joy, a splash of cheer,
Bright red droplets, sipping near.
Laughter bubbles, straw's delight,
Sunshine dances, oh what a sight!

Flavors burst like confetti toss,
Sipping slow, we're the boss.
Bubbles tickle, giggles fly,
Our silly drinks reach for the sky!

Frothy crowns on every head,
Juicy giggles, we're well-fed.
Mismatched straws in colors bright,
We sip on joy, pure and light!

Cheers to spills and fruity mess,
Each sip a treasure, we confess.
With every gulp, a burst of fun,
Our sunny party has begun!

A Palette of Nature's Candy

In the garden, colors clash,
Fruits are flying, oh what a splash!
Reds and purples, greens galore,
Each one waits, we can't ignore!

Munching on a rainbow treat,
Nature serves up something sweet.
With every bite, we dance and grin,
A fruity battle we are in!

Chasing flavors, oh what a race,
Juicy juices all over the place!
Sticky fingers, laughter wide,
Nature's pantry, our joy, our pride!

A caper here and a nibble there,
The taste explosion fills the air.
Painting smiles with each delight,
This sugary chaos feels just right!

Wild Wonders in the Meadow

In meadows green, where critters play,
Munching snacks throughout the day.
Bumblebees buzzing, skies so clear,
Funny faces, full of cheer!

Plump and round, they bounce around,
Nature's jellybeans abound.
Chasing butterflies, giggles soar,
Rolling in sweetness, we explore!

Popping berries in our mouth,
Happiness flowing from the south.
Dancing daisies, silly sights,
Meadow magic, pure delights!

With every step and every hop,
Juicy joy we just can't stop.
Laughter echoes, what a spree,
In this wild land, we're fancy-free!

Ripe Adventures Await

Trekking through the bushes wide,
Adventures wait on every side.
Fruits are hiding, come take a look,
Secrets tucked in nature's book!

Bumbling around, we laugh and climb,
Finding snacks, oh, it's snack time!
Nature's treasure hunt we embrace,
With berry smiles on every face!

Fruits like jewels, oh, what a win,
Squeezed in laughter, cider grin.
Chasing shadows, what a sight,
We leap and bound, feeling light!

At every twist, giggles ignite,
Juicy treasures, pure delight.
With every bite, a tale we weave,
In this ripe world, we believe!

www.ingramcontent.com/pod-product-compliance
Lightning Source LLC
Chambersburg PA
CBHW060141230426
43661CB00003B/519

Original title:
A Bowl of Peaches

Copyright © 2025 Creative Arts Management OÜ
All rights reserved.

Author: Christian Leclair
ISBN HARDBACK: 978-1-80586-266-6
ISBN PAPERBACK: 978-1-80586-738-8

Velvet Skin of Nature's Bounty

Round and plump, a sight to see,
Nature's gift, so ripe and free.
Snatch one up, but hold it tight,
Juicy joy, oh what a bite!

Watch them roll, they bounce and play,
Sticky fingers save the day.
Squirrels cheer and dance with glee,
Imagine peach pies, just for me!

Golden Gems of the Afternoon

Sun-kissed jewels on leafy beds,
Wobbling round like fluffy heads.
Grab a few, make quite a mess,
Laughter echoes, nothing less!

Time to juggle, feel the thrill,
Whack a friend, 'that's what they will!'
With each squish, a funny fight,
Rolling peaches, pure delight!

The Aroma of Peach Blossoms

Sweet perfume fills the warm, bright air,
Fragrance floats with playful flair.
Buzzing bees join in the fun,
Dance around till day is done!

A swirling waltz of floral grace,
Peachy magic in this place.
Under the sun, we spin and twirl,
With every scent, our laughter swirls!

Dripping Honey from the Tree

Golden drops in the summer heat,
Nature's candy, oh so sweet!
Sticky joy on fingers spread,
Giggles burst as we are fed!

The sun drips down, it starts to flow,
Mumbling friends call for a show.
Together we splash in a gooey spree,
With every spoon, more silliness, whee!

Fading Light of a Harvest Evening

In the orchard, shadows creep,
Fruit falling, no promise to keep.
A squirrel steals my glossy prize,
While I ponder where my last snack lies.

Friends gather, laughter fills the air,
One trips, sending peaches everywhere!
A sticky mess, a fruity fight,
Our evening ends with pure delight.

Cradle of Sweet Sensations

Round and round, we spin and dance,
As sweet treats lead us in a trance.
I take a bite, it slips away,
Who knew fruit could be so sly today?

Laughter bubbles, juice drips down,
Wearing pulp like a silly crown.
In the clumsiness, joy we find,
Making memories, sweetly entwined.

Murmurs of Fruit-Laden Branches

Branches sway, they shake and grin,
As if they're sharing secrets within.
A giggle hides among the leaves,
While I dodge bees like a game of thieves.

With one misplaced step, I lose my way,
Bumping into limbs that sway.
The fruit pauses, takes a breath,
As I laugh my way to fruity death.

Palettes of Golden Delicacies

Golden globes on sunlit lanes,
In colorful chaos, oh, what remains?
We launch our bounty, oh what a sight,
While laughing hard with all our might.

One's hat flies off, straight to the sky,
A peach lands softly, oh my, oh my!
We giggle, we squeal, as it rolls away,
In this silly game, we'll forever play.

Laughter Lingers in Orchard Breezes

In the orchard, giggles float,
As fruits begin their little boast.
"I'm sweeter than you," they all claim,
While squirrels watch, fueling the game.

Bees buzz by in a comical dance,
Hoping for a fruit-filled romance.
They twirl and fall, all in a rush,
Turning the orchard to a sweet hush.

The Season's Fickle Emotions

One day ripe, the next they pout,
Hiding behind leaves, scream and shout.
"Oh, who picked me first?" an apple cries,
While the peaches roll their worried eyes.

Rains come down, a fruit soap opera,
As laughter bubbles in a sweet tempo.
Cherry laughs, gets caught in a whirl,
While plums just stare, turning in a twirl.

Beneath the Leaves, a Hidden Joy

Under leaves, a giggle conceals,
As ripe fruit spins on merry wheels.
The grapes are rolling, having a blast,
Their laughter echoes, a sugary cast.

"Roots wiggle in, what a grand plot!"
Exclaims a cherry, quite the hotshot.
While tomatoes blush in radiant cheer,
Together they frolic without any fear.

When Warmth Meets Tenderness

Warm sunbeam tickles the trees with glee,
While fruits spin dreams of sweet jubilee.
Each peach is plotting a playful trick,
As the pears gather, quick and slick.

A little warmth makes mischief rise,
Ripened giggles under the big skies.
With a wink and twitch, they shout, "Surprise!"
As laughter lingers, the orchard sighs.

Sunkissed Bliss

Underneath the summer sun,
Fuzzy fruits come out to play,
They giggle as they roll around,
In their fruity, sweet ballet.

Juicy bites and sticky hands,
Laughter fills the sunlit air,
Who knew snacks could dance so well?
Oh, the joy is everywhere!

Sunkissed cheeks and silly grins,
As we feast upon the skin,
Beneath the trees, our laughter rings,
With every bite, another win!

A fruit-tastic, funny sight,
As we munch without a care,
Peachy dreams and silly schemes,
In this summer, oh so rare!

The Peach Melody

An orchestra of laughter plays,
With every crunch, a joyful sound,
Melodies of summer days,
Where fruity friends abound.

The sweet and tangy harmonize,
While we dance without a stop,
A pit here and a smile there,
On this fruity, fun-filled hop!

Each bite hits a perfect note,
As juices flow like summer rain,
In this juicy concert, we gloat,
With peachy rhythms in our veins.

A symphony of silly games,
As we twirl and spin so free,
In this tasty, fun parade,
Come join the peachy jubilee!

Harvested Dreams

In the orchard, mischief brews,
With plump delights just out of reach,
We strategize and share a ruse,
To nab our fruit without a speech.

With buckets full, we plot and scheme,
And giggles burst like bubbles bright,
For every peach, a silly dream,
Makes summer days a pure delight.

Juicy treasures in our hold,
With secret recipes in mind,
Little messes, tales retold,
Of fruity finds so well-defined.

Harvesting the laughs we share,
Each moment a sweet, funny stream,
In this orchard without a care,
We chase our ever-peachy dream!

Savoring the Summer Glow

Beneath the sun, we find our cheer,
As juicy globes take center stage,
Comedy in every smear,
While munching on this summer page.

Peach stains painted on our shirts,
Silly selfies, messy grin,
With every bite, our laughter spurts,
In this sweet, sun-kissed din.

A fruit disaster, who can tell?
As we frolic in the breeze,
With sticky fingers, all is well,
And summer's laughter never flees.

From trees to table, moments flow,
As sunbeams set our giggles free,
In every bite, a summer glow,
Funny times, just you and me!

In the Realm of Fuzzy Fruit

In fields of fuzz and sticky cheer,
The fruit parade begins each year.
Each plump delight, a jolly jest,
A shining orb, I must invest!

With peachy faces round and bright,
They giggle in the summer light.
I chase them down, they roll away,
These merry orbs, they've got to pay!

The squirrels all scheme, they plot and plan,
A peachy heist, oh what a scam!
I guard my loot, I play the game,
But in the end, all fruits are same!

With every bite, a juicy laugh,
I slip and slide, oh what gaffe!
In the realm of fuzzy fruit I find,
The silly joys that life designed.

The Lure of Juicy Independence

They dangle low, the ripe ones tease,
A sweet delight that aims to please.
With sticky fingers, oh what fun,
I'll claim my treasure from the sun!

The neighbors stare, they raise an eye,
As I leap high, I touch the sky.
One falls down, it lands with a thud,
And splat! Oh look, I'm covered in crud!

With every bite, the juice shoots free,
I parade around, oh look at me!
The fruit of freedom on my shirt,
A badge of honor – oh, what a dirt!

Independence calls with every drip,
From every juicy, wobbly nip.
So let them roll, let laughter reign,
This fruity freedom fuels my gain!

Sunset Hues in Citrus Clusters

In sunset hues, the clusters gleam,
A fruity palette, a painter's dream.
I reach for reds, and yellows too,
They beckon me, oh what a view!

But as I pluck, a slip I make,
One rolls away, oh what a break!
It zigzags past, my laugh's a shout,
Like citrus chaos, watch out, watch out!

With every bite, a burst of glee,
Sunset colors dance like me.
Juicy squirts and giggles start,
A fruity mishap – a work of art!

So gather 'round, let's share a slice,
With every smile, it's oh so nice.
In sunset hues, we'll make a fuss,
Together in this joyful bus!

Orchard Whispers in Summer's Lullaby

Beneath the trees, they softly sway,
Whispering sweet things all the day.
I listen close for secret calls,
As juicy laughter fills the halls!

A branch bows down, a gentle tease,
I reach to grab, but oh, my knees!
The ground approaches with a thump,
A peachy prize gets quite the jump!

Between the leaves, a giggle's heard,
A fruity choir sings without word.
I join the fun, I sway and twirl,
In orchard dreams, I gladly whirl!

So in this lullaby, I'll play,
With every squish, a bright bouquet.
Let summer's laughter fill the air,
An orchard's joy, beyond compare!

The Dance of Ripening Days

In the sun, they jiggle and sway,
Little orbs in a sunny ballet,
Peachy laughs in the warm, bright air,
Twisting and turning without a care.

The breeze joins in, gives a wink,
As flavors mingle, they dance and blink,
Each round shape boasts a juicy grin,
Inviting all to join in the spin.

Nature's humor, such sweet delight,
Silly fruits in their charming flight,
Watch them twirl, shine bright in the rays,
These sticky gems in a sunlit craze.

When harvest comes, who'll take the lead?
Chasing laughter, like kids with speed,
Together we sing, a joyful tune,
Under the welcoming afternoon moon.

A Tapestry of Orchard Promises

In orchards lush, where giggles grow,
Fruits blushing pink, putting on a show,
Each tree wears a dress of sweet surprises,
A comedy act in nature's disguises.

Plump little warriors, bold and bright,
Ready for plucking, what a sight,
With sticky fingers, we laugh and cheer,
For the harvest brings us near and dear.

A sticky handshake with the sun above,
Each bite a cuddle, a plush little hug,
Crimson cheeks and belly laughs abide,
As joy spills forth from every side.

Under the branches, we twirl and spin,
With silly faces and the fun we win,
A tapestry woven with laughter and cheer,
In this orchard spirit, we shed every fear.

Taste of Nectar on the Tongue

A juicy nibble, oh what a tease,
Exploding flavors that tickle and please,
Laughter erupts with every ripe bite,
A comedy sketch, a true delight.

Sweet nectar flows, and spills on the chin,
With giggles and grins, we merrily spin,
Each drop a jest, a playful trick,
Oh, what fun in our fruity pick!

Fruity fellows with grand, puffy cheeks,
Merrily munching, our laughter peaks,
In a garden of joy, we feast with glee,
Like clowns at a circus, just let it be.

When sweetness drips and we can't contain,
The joy turns wild, we'll never complain,
For in this game of flavors and fun,
We taste the joy of the golden sun.

Embracing All Things Sweet and Juicy

Gather 'round, let's toast with cheer,
To fruits that laugh, bringing us near,
Plump little wonders with a zest for joy,
Silly faces, like kids with a toy.

Each slice a giggle, every bite a tease,
The bounty of nature, sure to please,
In every mouthful, a party unfolds,
With humor and sweetness, a tale retold.

Chasing juice like kids in a race,
Sticky fingers and a playful embrace,
Nature's own jester, spinning so fine,
A carnival of flavors, oh how they shine!

So raise your glasses, to laughter and fun,
In the realm of sweetness, we're never done,
With every bright morsel, we dance and sing,
Embracing life's joy, it's a wonderful thing.

Nectar's Embrace beneath the Shade

In the garden, giggles bloom,
Chasing bees that dance and zoom.
One slipped on a fruit so round,
Splat! He landed with a sound.

We tangled in a peachy fight,
Laughter echoing delight.
Juices dripping from our chin,
Sticky sweetness, where to begin?

The Sweetness of Sun-Kissed Delights

What's that treasure in the sun?
A tasty laugh, oh what fun!
Each shiny orb, a playful tease,
Rolling down with such great ease.

We raced the wind, barely a care,
Tripping over fruit laid bare.
One by one, we hit the ground,
With laughter, we were tightly bound.

Juicy Reveries of the Harvest Moon

Under moonlight, a feast awaits,
Fragrant dreams on dessert plates.
Who knew that joy could be so grand,
When fruit plays games, unplanned.

We spun around with silly glee,
Each bite taken joyfully.
The stars chuckled, oh so bright,
Cheering us on, what a sight!

Sunkissed Orbs in a Woven Basket

A basket full of spinning spheres,
Packed with giggles, laughter, cheers.
One rolled off, a daring flight,
Prompting us to chase with might.

Peaches laughing as they fall,
Bouncing, rolling, one and all.
Our race became a fruity spree,
As we danced with glee, so free.

Honeyed Sunlight in a Tree's Embrace

In the branches high, a prankster waits,
Sunlight dripping through like honeyed fates.
Squirrels plotting in a furry debate,
Giggles echo, oh, what a wild state!

Birds chirp secrets, mischievous and sly,
Peachy surprises with each vibrant cry.
Nature's jesters, oh, they never shy,
A fruity fest is dancing in the sky!

The breeze sneezes, wafting scents so sweet,
Tickling noses, oh, what a treat!
These juicy gems make for a fun feat,
Laughter bounces on the warm, green seat!

Underneath the tree, we swing and sway,
Caught in giggles, in this peachy play.
With every bite, worries drift away,
Sun-kissed delight, who needs a bouquet?

Gentle Hands Hold Nature's Joy

Pick them gently, these orbs of pure cheer,
With each soft touch, laughter draws near.
Nature's plump gems, we hold them dear,
Juicy jokes pop, bringing joy sincere!

Mischief awaits in every ripe hue,
Slip on a slice, how clumsy we do!
Spilling their stories, like sunshine anew,
Silly moments, it's all we pursue!

Wrinkles of laughter line every face,
Messy as crumbs in this peachy race.
With sticky fingers, we find our place,
Joy in nature, oh, what a warm space!

When moonlight whispers, the fun's not done,
Silly songs echo, we dance and run.
In the arms of the night, we've all just begun,
These gentle treasures, oh, how we've won!

Where Color Meets Flavor

In this orchard, laughter paints the air,
With juicy bursts that prompt us to share.
Orange, yellow, pink everywhere,
Slicing through sweetness, flavor and flair!

We juggle our finds, like clowns on parade,
Fruits in the sun, oh, what a charade!
Splat goes the peach, on Grandma's aid,
Sticky giggles in our colorful trade!

Rolling downhill with our load of delight,
Peaches and laughter, what a funny sight!
In our fruit fort, everything feels right,
Nature's own party, day turns to night!

As the stars twinkle, the fun carries on,
With each fruity splash, a new joke's born.
In this rainbow patch, the worries are gone,
Where flavor and color are lovingly worn!

Lush Days of Abundant Sunshine

Sun-soaked mornings, bursting with glee,
Chasing flying fruits, oh, come catch me!
Slipping and sliding, how wild we be,
Lush and lovely, we dance, carefree!

Wiggling toes in the warm, grassy turf,
Every peach's chuckle brings forth a smurf.
Sticky friendship, it's certainly worth,
Nature's bounty, the best kind of mirth.

Rolling in laughter, catching the rays,
Peachy   games fill up all our days.
With every pluck, a new smile stays,
Under sunny skies, joy dilly-dally plays!

As twilight settles, stories unfold,
Lights of the evening like treasures of gold.
This orchard of laughter, tales never old,
Lush dreams in fruits, forever retold!

Aroma of Warmth and Wonder

In a kitchen sunny and bright,
A fruit parade brings sheer delight.
Chasing aromas, my stomach sings,
As peachy potions swirl on wings.

I step on toes, I dance with glee,
As juicy orbs roll free from me.
Hilarity strikes with every slip,
In this fruity, funny, scrumptious trip.

Sweetness Clothed in Fuzz

A fuzzy friend with a juicy grin,
Hiding treasure where smiles begin.
They wiggle and giggle in my palm,
Oh, sweet delight, so fuzzy and calm.

Impromptu feasts create quite the scene,
With juice that flows like a fruity stream.
Unleashed chaos as laughter grows,
With fuzzballs tumbling, nobody knows.

Gathered in the Light

Sunbeams catch a game of chase,
Fruity characters find their place.
A wobbly stack soon tips and falls,
Laughter erupts within these walls.

With arms outstretched, we catch and share,
These vibrant gems, beyond compare.
Who knew that fruit could spark such cheer?
A giggling bunch, we're full of joy here.

Parchment of Sunshine

Wrapped in warmth, a golden hue,
Of sweetness forged in laughter's brew.
I mismatched socks for a peachy feast,
Who needs a plate? I'm getting beast!

The sun makes aprons dance and sway,
While sticky fingers join in play.
In this silly fruit-filled spree,
I can't tell if it's lunch or me!

Fleshing Out the Sun

In a grove where giggles grow,
Juicy joys drop from trees below.
Plump and round, they sway with glee,
Nature's candy—come have a spree!

Lemonade laughs with every squeeze,
Their fluffy skins make summer tease.
A splash of juice, a dribble or two,
Oh, what fun these fruits can do!

When the day gets hot and bright,
Catch a snack and hold on tight.
Just beware, a slippery bite,
Can send you dancing, oh what a sight!

So gather round, friends, take your pick,
These plump prizes are quite the trick.
With a wink and a juicy grin,
Let the fruity fun begin!

Golden Orbs of Abundance

In the sun, they glow like gold,
Whispers of sweetness, tales untold.
Round and precious, they gleam in line,
Gather 'round for a taste divine!

With every bite, laughter erupts,
Drips and drops, we just can't stop.
Faces sticky, smiles wide,
In this fruity joy, we take pride!

Splat goes a juicy surprise,
As a fruit rolls, oh what a rise!
Chasing orbs in a playful race,
Are you ready for this fun embrace?

So join the feast, don't be shy,
These golden gems will make you fly!
With belly aches from all the cheer,
We'll munch until the end is near!

The Essence of Ripeness

With a wink, they beckon near,
Chubby morsels full of cheer.
Giggling fruits with juicy smiles,
Are here to charm us for a while!

A bite reveals a daring splash,
Getting sticky in a flash.
In this fruit-filled comedy show,
Laughter rises high, just let it flow!

Chasing sweetness with delight,
Stumbling here, a comical sight.
Fruits unite to bring pure joy,
What fun we find, oh girl and boy!

So toss a peach, spin a dream,
This is better than it may seem.
Life's sweeter with this fruity spree,
Let's caper on with glee and glee!

Sun-Kissed Treasures

Beneath the sky, they twinkle bright,
Sun-kissed baubles, pure delight.
Plucking moments, laughter spills,
Too many fruits, and time stands still!

Bright and bulging with each cheer,
A fruity brawl, the end is near!
Rolling, bouncing, in a heap,
Splat! Oh, let's take a leap!

In the shade, we gather round,
With juicy prizes that we've found.
Face to face, a playful feast,
From the playful to the least!

So raise your fruits and cheer aloud,
For nature's bounty, we are proud!
With giggles shared and sticky hands,
Let's revel in these wondrous lands!

Serenity Found in a Peach Orchard

Amidst the trees where shadows play,
A plump delight beckons each day.
With laughter bright and sunlit cheer,
I'd climb for joy, not out of fear.

Each peach a treasure, soft and round,
With friends to share, together found.
We toss the fruit, it flies through air,
It's peachy chaos everywhere!

Sticky fingers, grins so wide,
Juicy joy we cannot hide.
A few we munch, a few we toss,
In this ripe field, we're all the boss!

As sunset paints the sky in gold,
Our laughter echoes, stories told.
In every bite, our worries cease,
As we indulge, we find our peace.

Yonder, a Glimpse of Heaven's Nectar

With fuzzy friends and sunny dreams,
The orchard whispers joyful screams.
I roll a peach down hill with glee,
It's nature's game, come play with me!

A fruit parade, we dance and twirl,
Juicy jests with every swirl.
One slips and lands upon my shoe,
Who knew a peach could also chew?

In bounty bright, the laughter flows,
Dribbled juice, our faces glow.
With every bite, our spirits sing,
Oh, what joy these soft fruits bring!

So gather 'round, let's munch and chat,
In this sweet haven, we all sit fat.
For every peach is pure delight,
In this orchard, everything's bright!

Sunlit Paths and Juicy Joys

Wandering down sunlit lanes,
Where succulent magic never wanes.
With laughter loud, I grab a few,
These fruity wonders, bright and true.

A peach plops down, oh what a splash!
It's peachy chaos in a dash!
I stumble back, what a wild sight,
These jolly fruits bring pure delight!

With sticky hands, we share a bite,
Each juicy morsel, sheer delight.
The flavors dance upon our tongue,
In orchard fun, we're all so young!

From branches high, the fruits do swing,
While laughter flows, we dance and sing.
In this warm sun, our hearts do play,
In juicy joys, we find our way!

The Poetry of Ripe Fruit

In shadows cast by branches wide,
A symphony of joy resides.
With peaches ripe, I start to rhyme,
In fruity verses, we taste the time.

Beneath the leaves, we laugh and shout,
Each squishy bite, we can't live without.
The sticky juice drips down my chin,
In this grand feast, we all win!

With friends at hand, we make a mess,
A juicy battle, who's more blessed?
The orchard sings in fruity cheer,
In every moment, the fun is clear!

So let us cherish this playful spree,
Where fruits abound, we feel so free.
In laughter's embrace, our hearts take flight,
For the poetry found is pure delight!

Sweet Summer Harvest

Peaches rolling down the hill,
Chasing them takes quite the skill.
Sunshine laughs, the nectar's sweet,
Watch your step or slip on your feet.

Juicy fruits in every hand,
Giggles shared across the land.
Sticky fingers, summer's prize,
Who knew fruit could bring such sighs?

Nectar on the Tongue

Sipping nectar like a king,
Fruit juice dribbling, what a fling!
Wobbly chairs, some peachy bites,
Sunburned noses, summer lights.

A fuzzy skin catches my eye,
Caught in peachy espionage spy.
Slipping, sliding, what a game,
"Oops!" they shout, and I feel fame.

Orchard's Delight

In the orchard, what a sight,
Peachy giggles taking flight.
Baskets dangling from our arms,
Who needs charm when fruit disarms?

Under trees, we laugh and play,
Counting bites, we lose the day.
If you drop one, chase it fast!
Is that a peach, or did it blast?

Juicy Whispers of Summer

Whispers sweet as summer's sun,
Peaches hide and then they run!
A race to catch the squishy treat,
Juicy bites, a summer feat.

When the laughter starts to flow,
Watch the fruit, it steals the show!
Mischief mingles with the breeze,
No one minds the sticky knees.

A Tangy Embrace

In the orchard where the sun does beam,
A fruit so plump, it bursts at the seam.
I took a bite, oh what a thrill,
Juice dripped down, and oh, what a spill!

The neighbors laughed, they gathered 'round,
As I danced, my feet left the ground.
With sticky hands, and a cheeky grin,
I claimed my crown as the peach-slim king!

The dogs rushed in, for a fruity feast,
While I sat there, sticky, to say the least.
They sniff and slobber, oh what a scene,
A wild peach party, fit for a queen!

But as I feasted, I felt it too,
A belly rumble, the fruit's bold brew.
So with a grin, I made my retreat,
In the land of peaches, I admit defeat!

The Essence of Sweetness

In a basket, round and bright,
Sits a treasure, quite the sight.
Soft and fuzzy, oh what a treat,
Every bite is pure, sublime sweet!

I took a risk, a daring dive,
To taste the flavor that comes alive.
Spitting pits became my sport,
With each toss, laughter's consort!

My friends all cheered, a jovial crew,
As I juggled fruit, just for the view.
One wobbled down, a slip, a fall,
Now it's my turn to be the clown of the hall!

Smeared with juices, I stand with pride,
In this fruity chaos, we joyfully glide.
Every bite brings laughter, so profound,
The essence of sweetness, joy unbound!

Fields of Tenderness

In fields where the sunlight dances free,
A fuzzy fruit can't help but tease.
I waltzed among the trees so spry,
Until a peach fell and flew right by!

It knocked my hat right off my head,
A silly hat, just like I said!
With laughter echoing, around I twirled,
A peachy ballet, oh what a world!

The bees did buzz, the birds did sing,
As I dodged the fruit that made my heart sing.
With every splash of sunshine's glow,
I pranced through orchards, feeling the flow!

And though I tripped, with joy, I rolled,
Nestled in laughter, bright and bold.
In fields of tenderness, I found my glee,
With juicy stars, life's jubilee!

Spheres of Ambrosia

In the market, oh what a sight,
Spheres of glory, in colors bright.
I reached for one, oh what a tease,
It rolled away with whimsical ease!

I chased it down, a playful race,
But that peach had quite the grace.
Bumping through carts, it made its escape,
While I, the fool, tried to reshape!

A vendor laughed, said, "Come get your prize!"
As the peach danced on, full of surprise.
A tumble here, a joyful shout,
Those spheres of ambrosia spark true clout!

Finally caught, I took a bite,
Sweetness burst forth, pure delight.
In that moment, oh what cheer,
The chase was worth it, never fear!

Ripe Reflections in Sunlight's Glow

In the orchard, I took a stroll,
Peaches hanging like a loose control.
One fell down, gave me a scare,
A fruit ninja had picked from the air!

With a juicy splash, my shirt got stained,
At least I wasn't the one who complained.
Spinning around like a carefree bee,
Chasing shadows, feeling so free!

I blurted, 'Hey, aren't clouds made of fluff?'
Then I dodged a peach; man, this is tough!
Laughter echoed as my friend took aim,
Trying to catch me—oh, what a game!

But every bite's sweet, juicy, and bright,
Even dodging fruit feels just right.
In this playground of sticky delight,
We'll giggle 'til stars fill the night!

A Symphony of Stone-Fruit Dreams

In a world of nectar and zest so divine,
I blurted, 'These fruits? They should really be wine!'
Each plump delight, a perfect façade,
Tasting heaven, but a pit is my lawn guard!

The fruit band played with its juicy refrain,
Bananas on drums, I can't stay sane.
Watermelons crooned with a sweet, silly cheer,
While lemons danced, swaying with beer!

A giggle erupted; a peach took a leap,
Turns out fruits have secrets they keep.
With every bite, the jokes just grew,
This fruity fest was my dream come true!

So let's toast to flavors both funny and sly,
As the nectar drips down, we can't pass by.
In this fruity concert, together we sing,
Finding joy in the ripe, the laughter it brings!

Rustic Charm of the Fruit Stand

At the local stand, I spotted the loot,
A mountain of stones wrapped up in fruit.
The vendor cackled, tossing me a pear,
Said, 'Watch out! These lovelies bite, I swear!'

My friend grabbed a peach, with a cheeky grin,
Squeezed it tight, and it burst right in.
Juice sprayed everywhere, what a mess!
We laughed and swore, 'This is pure finesse!'

A line of customers, they stood with delight,
As I danced with swirls of juice in full sight.
'Next time be careful,' they all did jest,
But oh, how I love a messy fruit fest!

In this quaint charm, where joy's misconstrued,
Every bite is shared, laughter renewed.
Rustic peaches, perfection in hand,
At this fruit stand, we make merry and stand!

Sweet Illusions of Late August

In late August, the sun starts to fade,
Peaches glow bright, like a sweet charade.
Each one a treasure, mischievous delight,
They giggle and wink, oh, what a sight

Chasing sunlight, they roll with glee,
While bees buzz around, all slappy-happy.
A peach rolled too far, it caused quite a scene,
As I tripped and tumbled, feeling like a queen!

With sticky fingers, we managed a snack,
Creating a mess, there's no turning back.
Juice dribbled down, all over my chin,
These fruity follies make us laugh and grin!

So here's to the summer, sweet mischief in tow,
In a world of fruit, where laughter can grow.
Late August shines bright, with flavors so grand,
We'll savor the moments, hand in sticky hand!

Petals and Stone: An Evening's Tale

In the garden where laughter grows,
The fruits dance like a band of pros.
A peach took a twirl, quite bold,
Said, "I've got stories yet untold!"

The daisies chuckled, petals bright,
While bees buzzed in a sweet delight.
"Come join our waltz, don't be shy!"
But the peach just winked and said, "Oh my!"

Tonight's not for dancing, I fear,
I'm too ripe, and it's too near.
But just wait until the first slice,
Then I'll be smooth and oh so nice!"

With giggles and glee, they spun the night,
Under a moon that shone so bright.
A tale of sweet fruits, laughter, glee,
In the garden of whimsy, wild and free.

Odes to the Golden Harvest

Upon the tree, a treasure hangs,
With golden hues from vine it sprang.
A soft breeze whispers, "Oh what fun!"
Let's munch these gems 'til day is done!

The squirrels gather with tiny hands,
Claiming their share of the fruity lands.
"One for you, and two for me!"
Mischief blooms with every spree!

The plumpest peach was quite the catch,
"I make the best pie—it's a perfect match!"
But alas, one slip sent him down,
And landed him with quite a frown!

As laughter echoed, they gathered near,
To taste the spoils of their fruitful cheer.
With crumbs and juice, the evening's lost,
In a feast where laughter is the cost!

Sunshine Caught in Juicy Flesh

Oh, the sun dripped golden rays,
Onto fruit where sweetness stays.
A juicy tale of bold delight,
With every bite, the world feels right!

A crew of critters, all aligned,
With juicy plans that are unconfined.
"Let's make a sauce!" shouted a bee,
"Or maybe jam for you and me!"

But with each scoop and silly splash,
They tumbled into a juicy mash.
A bouncy ball of laughter met,
As sticky paws turned friends to pets!

By evening's end, they rolled in zest,
With smiles wider than a nest.
For every fruit's a spark of joy,
In this harvest dance, no soul's a toy!

Crimson Clouds Over Sweet Gardens

Beneath the sky, a riot blooms,
With blushy cheeks and fruity grooms.
A peach pranced 'neath the crimson light,
Said, "Let's party deep into the night!"

The ants lined up with tiny mugs,
Claiming the drinks, just like chubby bugs.
"I'll toast to the juicy good times here!"
Laughter bubbled; that's the cheer!

But suddenly a breeze took hold,
Turning our feast a bit too bold.
With slipping fruits and wild delight,
They rolled beneath stars, stars so bright!

As giggles spread and stories soared,
Each fruit was cherished, every word adored.
With sweetened heavens dancing high,
They feasted 'til the night said goodbye!

Capturing Time in Sweet Spheres

Juicy orbs upon the tree,
Hanging low and feeling free.
One slips down, it starts to roll,
Chasing dreams, oh what a goal!

Fruitful laughter fills the air,
A sticky hand, a peach to share.
Friends unite in fruity cheer,
Who knew that fun was so near?

Sticky giggles, oh what fun,
Waiting for the setting sun.
In this moment, we all shine,
Nature's candy, truly divine!

Let's indulge in every bite,
Life's too short to fuss and fight.
So grab a peach, let's make a mess,
Life's a game, we must confess!

A Canvas of Ripening Sunsets

Brushstrokes of orange, yellow, red,
Each peach a story, gently spread.
Bite into colors, taste the hues,
Savoring laughter, joy, and views.

Nature's palette on display,
Funny faces in clay today.
We paint our lives with juicy treats,
Taking bites while dodging bees' feats.

A surprise squirt, oh what a thrill,
Unexpected juice, a tarty spill.
We laugh and dance, we twirl around,
Our silly antics, oh so profound!

As dusk descends with peachy glee,
We raise our cups of fruity tea.
In this canvas, let's create,
Funny memories, sealed by fate!

Scented Sorrows Beneath the Boughs

Underneath the leafy shade,
Scented whispers seem to fade.
But wait! A peach falls from above,
It's just a prank, oh what a love!

With every bite, we laugh and sigh,
Even when our juice runs dry.
A pitty surprise, we'll call it fate,
Such sweet chaos, let's celebrate!

Sorrow drips, like sticky rain,
Yet joy can blossom amidst the pain.
A fruity tear, a giggle too,
Life's a puzzle, with flavors anew.

So here we sit, with sticky hands,
Among the greens, our silly plans.
Let's chase away each heavy thought,
In fruity laughter, we find what's sought!

Musings on a Lazy Afternoon

Sunshine bright, and peaches ripe,
Silly thoughts, they swirl and type.
A fruit fight breaks out, hooray,
As laughter leads our minds astray.

Sitting back, we spill the tea,
Covered in juice, we're wild and free.
Just one more peach, we can't resist,
With every bite, we add to the list.

Plans for summer drift like clouds,
Peach-fueled dreams, we shout out loud.
Let's tumble down this juicy trail,
Where every giggle finds a sail.

Afternoons spent in golden bliss,
Fruity fun, who needs a kiss?
In sticky joy, we spend our day,
With vibrant thoughts, come what may!

A Feast of Sun-Drenched Marvels

On sunny days, we gather round,
With laughter loud, and joy profound.
The fruit so ripe, a treat to share,
A sticky mess, without a care.

Giggles echo in the breeze,
Juicy bites that bring us ease.
We juggle seeds and wear the juice,
In this delightful, silly ruse.

With faces smeared in shades of gold,
The tales we tell, never get old.
Each peach a gem, a treasure piled,
We eat like pirates, giggling, wild!

So raise a slice to summer's bliss,
With every bite, we share a kiss.
We'll feast until the sun goes down,
In our peachy kingdom, we wear the crown.

Savoring Life's Soft Delights

We crouch on grass, the sun ablaze,
With juicy fruits, we bask and graze.
A drippy joy, like sticky hugs,
Our fingers dance with sweetish jugs.

The neighbors gawk, they think we're nuts,
With faces full of peachy guts.
We're in a sticky, playful trance,
A fruit-filled, juicy, summer dance!

Each bite a laugh, a giggle, a cheer,
In our fruity realm, there's naught to fear.
With every drip, our woes disappear,
In the realm of softness, we persevere.

So let them stare, we're here for fun,
In the joy of peaches, we've already won.
With laughter echoing through the trees,
We savor life's sweet, tender breeze.

The Color of a Summer Memory

Deep in the yard, a treasure waits,
With colors bright, it captivates.
A flash of orange, gold, and blush,
The sunlight calls, we cannot rush.

We gather close, a merry crew,
With cheeky grins and bellies too.
The juice will splatter, oh what fun!
Summer smiles, we're never done!

Like painters bold, we mix and smear,
What flavor's best? We disagree here!
A sip, a slurp, the chaos flows,
In this delicious, joyful prose.

Moments like this, they stick with you,
With every giggle, we paint anew.
In peachy hues, we live and thrive,
These memories, they keep us alive.

Whispers of Warm Winds and Sweetness

In warm winds' hush, the giggles rise,
With mushy fruits, we're in for surprise.
The sweet aroma calls us near,
With fragrant laughter filling the cheer.

A slip, a slide, it's all in play,
A joyful mess, we'll save the day!
The taste of summer, a fruity tease,
Dancing boldly in the trees.

Who thought a bite could spark such glee?
The sticky fun brings harmony.
In shades of yellow, orange, and red,
We savor life with every spread.

In our peachy world, absurd and bright,
With playful hearts roaming the night.
So here's to laughter, oh what a treat,
In the whispers of sweetness, we're never discreet.

Fields of Gold and Orchard Dreams

In the orchard where laughter lives,
Each fruit a prank, a joke it gives.
With every bite, a giggle pops,
Sweet juice drips, and humor hops.

What's sneaky and yellow? Guess it right!
A peach in disguise, a funny sight.
Beware of pits, they tend to prank,
Like little ninjas, they move with rank.

In fields of gold, we dance and play,
Each peach a tale of a silly day.
With every chuckle, the sun shines bright,
Who knew fruit could bring so much light?

So gather 'round, let the laughter flow,
With fuzz and sweetness, steal the show.
In these orchards, joy can't be beat,
With every bite, it's pure, fruity treat.

Radiant Pomology

In the land of fruit, where jokes grow tall,
An apple's a jester, having a ball.
Peaches wear wigs made of fuzzy delight,
As pears throw a party, oh what a sight!

Mangoes are prancing in sunlit glee,
Zesty little characters, wild and free.
Cucumbers tell tales of their wacky crew,
While cherries burst forth with their sweet debut!

Oh, the colors, the flavors, a carnival show,
With laughter and giggles, we reap what we sow.
In radiant rows, they shine like a star,
Fruit laughter echoes, near and far!

So come take a bite, join in the fun,
In this pomology, there's room for everyone.
With each fruity whisper, a chuckle is near,
Join the frolic, let's all share the cheer!

Bittersweet Breaths of Late Summer

In the dusk of summer, we breathe in the beat,
With fruits nostalgic, both sour and sweet.
Juicy whispers tease the warm, balmy air,
Each fruit a character, beyond compare.

The plums hold secrets, perhaps they're shy,
While grapefruits laugh, they always comply.
"Take a zest of life!" the lemons chime in,
With bitter-sweet stories, where laughter can begin.

Oh, the laughter mingles with summer's breath,
As we toast to fruits, even grapefruits' death!
Memories flicker, like fireflies dance,
In fields of laughter, let's take our stance.

So let's celebrate this twilight delight,
In the glow of the harvest, the peachy twilight.
With smiles and quirks, we'll raise a cheer,
To absurd little fruits throughout the year!

When Summer's Heart is Full

When summer's heart is a pump of fun,
Fruits fool around under the sultry sun.
With every bite, there's whimsy to find,
A sweet little prank for the open mind.

Bananas slip on their yellow peels,
While cherries chatter with quirky appeals.
Melons throw parties, greens make a scene,
What a fruit circus, so vivid and keen!

As the season fades to a colorful hum,
Let's dance with squashes, feel the fun drum.
With silly delights, our hearts become full,
In this fruity fiesta, life's never dull.

So gather the laughter, lift up your cheer,
In this summer orchard, good times appear.
With each juicy giggle, we bask in the light,
When summer's heart shines, everything feels right!

Lush Laughter in the Shade

Under the tree, giggles burst,
Fruit plops down, oh what a first!
Sticky fingers, faces bright,
Nature's candy, pure delight.

Squirrels stare with jealous eyes,
These round orbs, our sweet disguise.
We try to eat, but they escape,
Dancing around in juicy shape.

The Allure of Succulent Breaths

Biting in, a squirt goes wide,
Laughter spills, we cannot hide.
Each munch brings a fruity zing,
Watch out! Here comes that sticky fling!

Friends gather for a picnic feast,
Where laughter flows, and worries cease.
Smooth and round, we take a chance,
With each slip, we start to dance.

Translucent Skin, Hidden Sweetness

Playful shapes greet the hot sun,
With secret sweetness just for fun.
Our cheeks a mess, oh what a sight,
Who knew eating could feel so right?

They roll away, but we get sly,
Laughter echoes, oh my, oh my!
Nestled low, they're hard to find,
We chase them down, no peace of mind.

Ode to the Juicy Gem

A treasure hunt beneath green leaves,
Found a gem, and oh how it weaves!
Juicy bliss, a burst, a squirt,
We make a frenzied, tasty flirt.

Each bite brings giggles, can't resist,
Who knew fruit could be like this?
With every munch, the fun ascends,
In this fruity joy, our day transcends.

Tales from the Orchard Path

In the orchard, fruit does talk,
Gossiping kids as they walk.
"I'm the sweetest, can't you see?"
"Nah, my juice is the key!"

Squirrels roll and claim their prize,
Chasing dreams beneath the skies.
One forgets, beneath the tree,
A peach escapes, oh woe is me!

The bees buzz loud, they know their role,
While rabbits hop with jolly stroll.
Each nibble brings a funny face,
As sticky hands find their embrace!

Even clouds seem to drop by,
To taste the fruits, oh my, oh my!
With every bite, laughter rings
Among the orchards' silly things.

Rippling Reflections of Dusk

Sunsets in the orchard dance,
Peaches sport a sun-kissed glance.
They giggle as the shadows play,
In tones of gold, they make their way!

Beneath the trees, a picnic spread,
With fruits that sing, and laughter led.
Friends toss a peach with glee,
While dancing llamas sip their tea!

The breeze whispers silly tunes,
As fireflies waltz beneath the moons.
One peach trips, rolls on the grass,
Declares, "Catch me! Now I'll pass!"

Oh, laughter echoes in the air,
As dusk prepares its cozy chair.
With flavors rich, and hearts so free,
This orchard holds a jubilee!

The Weight of Morning Dew

Morning dew on leaves so bright,
A silly game in morning light.
Peaches giggle, plump and round,
While ants dance on the leafy ground.

Each droplet sings a sparkling song,
As they hop and twirl along.
One round fruit, under a leaf,
Cries out, "Dew, you're such a thief!"

Frogs jump high, they join the fun,
Sipping nectar, on the run.
With smiles wide and dreams so bold,
They share their secrets, sweet and gold.

As morning breaks, with joy they soar,
Weightless laughter, forevermore.
In every drop, a peachy wink,
Nature's jesters, what do you think?

Flavors Found in Nature's Secrets

Under boughs, the flavors blend,
Crops of giggles never end.
Each bite holds a story's grace,
In every corner, a funny face!

Bees with hats, they sip and sing,
While owls pass round the peachy bling.
A rolling fruit with arms outstretched,
Calls to friends, "This game's well fetched!"

Ripe laughter ripens with the sun,
A secret recipe, shared by fun.
With every taste, a chuckle spills,
Nature's joy, the heart it fills.

Underneath the old oak's dome,
The flavors make the orchard home.
With winks and smiles in every dish,
Just one bite, and it's pure bliss!

Slivers of Summer's Fare

Juicy globes in sun's warm glow,
A slippery treasure, oh so slow.
Squirrels dance, they take their chance,
In a wild and fruity romanced glance.

Pit spills seeds all over the place,
Sticking to my fingers; oh, what a race!
Sticky smiles and laughter loud,
Worms have parties in the crowd.

Juice drips down my chin, quite neat,
While onlookers cheer to the beat.
Too much fun with every bite,
I'll need a towel, oh what a sight!

Endless pranks, so sweet and slick,
Who knew fruit could play such a trick?
With every chew, a giggle slips,
Growing a garden of silly quips.

Abundant Splendor

A treasure trove of sunlit delight,
Bouncing off the ground, quite a sight.
I trip and tumble, what a mess,
Yet laughter rules, I must confess.

Fuzzy balls roll away with grace,
Chasing them feels like a race.
Giggles echo as we chase,
Who's the fastest in this odd place?

Dance with strangers, twirl away,
Making jams is just a play.
Sweet tunes of laughter fill the air,
While we all become fruit-stuffed bears.

Jam spills over, our fingers snag,
Bottoms up for the fruity swag!
A splendor shared, each mishap grand,
Together we face the sticky band.

Beneath the Peach Tree

Underneath the leafy crown,
Sneaky squirrels jump up and down.
Every peach is a little plunder,
While we feast in this fruity wonder.

Tangled toes in fallen fruit,
Cousins argue who gets the loot.
With each crunch, a giggle flies,
Adding sweetness to our cries.

A burst of flavor makes us grin,
Stuck in this game, we all win!
Splattered shirts, what a sight,
With juicy laughter, we feel light.

Oh, the chaos, oh, the fun,
Under the tree, we are all one.
Sun-kissed faces, smiles so wide,
In this crazy fruit-filled ride.

Nature's Sweet Offering

Nature calls with a cheeky smile,
Fluffy clouds stretch a while.
Sweet little orbs on the ground,
Each one holds a giggle, round.

Pits and giggles weave a tale,
Running feet on earthy trail.
A bumpy ride, hold on tight,
As fruits escape in pure delight.

Laughter bubbles in the air,
Who knew fruit could cause a scare?
With our hair a sticky mess,
We laugh at nature's pure finesse.

Snack attack, what a show,
Faced with fruit, it's all aglow.
With every bite, joy we find,
In nature's jest, we're intertwined.

www.ingramcontent.com/pod-product-compliance
Lightning Source LLC
Chambersburg PA
CBHW060141230426
43661CB00003B/514